Rainl

Canadian Health Activities G

MW00571123

Encouraging Topic Interest

Help students to develop an understanding and appreciation for different health concepts. Engage students through stories, non-fiction books, videos, posters, and other resources as a springboard for learning.

Black Line Masters and Graphic Organizers

Encourage students to use the black line masters and graphic organizers to present information, reinforce important concepts and to extend opportunities for learning. The graphic organizers will help students focus on important ideas, or make direct comparisons.

Learning Logs

Keeping a learning log is an effective way for students to organize their thoughts and ideas about the health concepts presented. Student learning logs also give the teacher insight on what follow up activities are needed to review and to clarify concepts learned.

Learning logs can include the following kinds of entries:

- Teacher prompts
- Student personal reflections
- Questions that arise
- Connections discovered
- Labeled diagrams and pictures

Culminating Activity: Create A Health Magazine

Have students demonstrate what they have learned about health, by creating a Kids Health Magazine. This culminating activity can be done as a whole class project, in small groups or independently. Encourage students to browse through magazines to get ideas. Student checklists are included.

Rubrics and Checklists

Use the rubrics and checklists in this book to assess student learning.

Table of Contents

Chalkboard Publishing Inc © 2007

Canadian Health Activities Grades 4-6

All About Me Activity Ideas

Activity Idea: Websites About Growing Up

Puberty is the transitional time between childhood and adulthood. The changes that occur during puberty do not happen over a strict time line. Instead it is unique for each child. This can be a very difficult and confusing time for children. Here are some excellent websites about growing up and the stages of puberty.

http://www.childdevelopmentinfo.com/development/puberty.htm

This website gives excellent information for parents on how to share information with their child.

http://www.kidshealth.org/kid/grow/body_stuff/puberty.html

Encourage students to learn more about what might be or will be happening to their bodies. This website is written in kid friendly language and has an abundant amount of information.

Extension Ideas:

- Introduce a question box where students could ask questions anonymously.
- Discuss with students the benefits, opportunities, challenges, and responsibilities of growing up.

Activity Idea: My Strengths And Weaknesses

Have students complete a web graphic organizer to show their strengths and another web to show things they think they need to improve on. Reinforce the ideas that everyone has strengths and weaknesses.

Discussion Starters:

- How do you feel when you do something well?
- Do you think it is o.k. to have things to improve on?
- Pick one thing you would like to improve. What are the steps in order to improve?

Activity Idea: The People In Your Life

Encourage students to think about the people in their life. Have students think how people are close to you for different reasons.

Discussion Starters:

- Who are the most important people in your life? Why?
- Who are the people that make you feel special or important?
- Who can you go to if you have a problem?
- Do you think it is important to let your family know if you are feeling upset, angry or anxious about something? Explain your thinking
- Would you speak to a friend the same way you would speak to your parent(s)? Why?

Activity Idea: Dealing With Peer Pressure

As a whole group, discuss peer pressure – pressure from people your own age to do things you normally wouldn't do on your own. Peer pressure can be both positive and negative. Create a class T- Chart and list examples of both positive and negative peer pressure.

Discussion Starters:

- Why do you think people like to belong to a group?
- What does it take to stand up against negative peer pressure?
- Have you ever experienced negative peer pressure where you almost or did do something you did not want to do? If so, what happened and how did it make you feel?
- Have you ever experienced positive peer pressure where you tried something new? If so, what happened and how did it make you feel?

Introducing...

Create a collage using pictures, words, or symbols clipped from magazines that represent things about you, things you enjoy doing, places you have visited, people you admire, and things you like about yourself.

One of the things I like about myself is...

Chalkboard Publishing Inc © 2007

Canadian Health Activities Grades 4-6

Student Interview

Interview a fellow student in the class.

Student Interview

Name _____

Date of Birth _____ Grade _____

a. List 3 words to describe you.

b. What is your favourite colour?

c. What is your favoutrite food?

d. What is your favourite movie?

e. What is your favourite book?

f. What is your favourite activity outside of school?

g. What activity do you dislike?

h. Who is a person you admire a lot? Explain.

i. What do you want to be when you grow up?

j. Where is a place you would like to visit someday?

Chalkboard Publishing Inc © 2007

Canadian Health Activities Grades 4-6

A Time Line

Create a time line to show the important events in your life.

	Age	Important Event
1.		
2.		
3.		
4.		
5.		
6.		
7.		
8.		

Canadian Health Activities Grades 4-6

Changes or Milestones in Your Life

In the chart below, identify a change or a milestone in your life. An example might be moving to another place or getting a new pet.

1. **What was a change in your life?**

2. **What happened after the change?**

3. **How did you feel about the change?**

Chalkboard Publishing Inc © 2007

Canadian Health Activities Grades 4-6

Circle of the People in Your Life

Think about the people in your life. Put your name in the center circle. Next, place names of immediate family members, relatives, friends and other people in your life in the circles around you. If you feel close to a person write their name in a circle nearest to you. As you feel less close to a person, write their name in a circle further away from you.

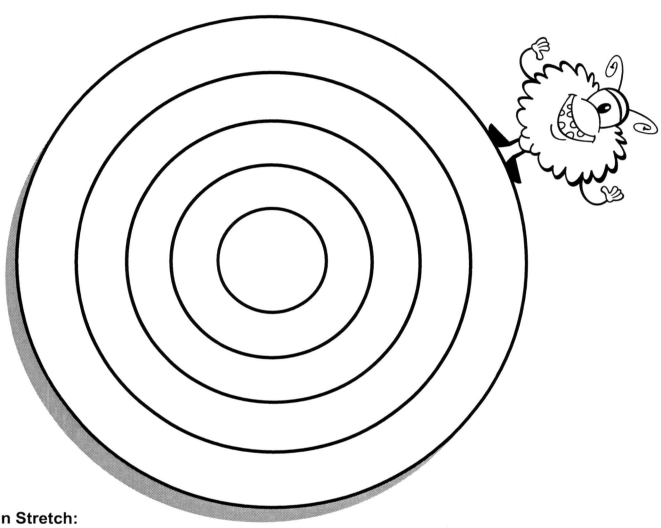

1. **Brain Stretch:**

Look at your circle of people. Why did you make some of your choices?

_____

_____

Do you think your circle of people could ever change? Explain.

_____

_____

_____

Chalkboard Publishing Inc © 2007

Canadian Health Activities Grades 4-6

Getting Along With Others

People get along better when they cooperate and listen to each other. Take the survey and think about how well you get along with others.

Cooperation Skills	Always	Sometimes	Never
1. I share with others.			
2. I take turns			
3. I take responsibility for my share of group work.			
4. I give compliments when someone is doing well.			
5. I talk about disagreements and problem solve.			
6. I invite people to join a group.			

Listening Skills	Always	Sometimes	Never
1. I listen to others without interrupting.			
2. I concentrate on what the speaker is saying.			
3. I ask questions to ensure understanding or to find out more.			
4. I look at the person while they speaking.			
5. I can repeat what someone says accurately.			

Listening Skills	Always	Sometimes	Never
1. I speak clearly.			
2. I look at the person I am speaking to.			
3. I speak loud enough so people can hear me.			

Chalkboard Publishing Inc © 2007

Canadian Health Activities Grades 4-6

Brain Stretch: Getting Along With Others

1. Review your responses. How would you rate your "getting along with others skills'? Explain.

_____

_____

_____

_____

2. In what way do you need to improve?

_____

_____

_____

_____

3. How do you think you can you use these skills in everyday life?

_____

_____

_____

_____

4. Why do you think it is easier to get along with some people rather than others?

_____

_____

_____

_____

Chalkboard Publishing Inc © 2007

Canadian Health Activities Grades 4-6

Family Members Work Together

Think about your role in your family. How do you contribute? How do you help?
Complete the chart to show how each family member contributes to help work together.

Family Member	Job or Contribution

Brain Stretch:

What would happen if your family did not work together? Explain.

Canadian Health Activities Grades 4-6

Likenesses and Differences

Everyone can have likenesses and differences. Find people in your class who:

• has the same favourite colour as you	• is taller than you	• was born in another town or city	• has a different birthday month than you
• likes to do art activities	• has the same colour eyes.	• takes some kind of lessons	• has a pet.
• has the same birthday month as you	• doesn't have a pet	• plays an instrument	• can speak another language
• is shorter than you	• likes vegetables	• is wearing blue jeans	• is the same height

Chalkboard Publishing Inc © 2007

Canadian Health Activities Grades 4-6

Be An Advice Columnist

Pretend you are the advice columnist for a kids' health magazine. Read the following letters and write a letter of advice for each.

Dear Advisor,

My friends have told me that I have to steal something in order to be in their special group. If I don't do it, they say they won't be my friends.

I want them to still be my friends, but I don't want to steal!

What should I do?

Dear Advisor,

My friend wants me to try out for the school soccer team with her.

I really like to play soccer, but I don't want to embarrass myself.

What should I do?

Dear Advisor,

All my friends have already kissed somebody. I feel like I am the only one left. I don't feel like I belong around my friends. All they do is talk about kissing.

Should I just kiss someone to get it over with?

What should I do?

Dear Advisor,

I really want to be in the school choir. My friends say I have a great voice and should try out. My friends said they would come with me and try out too.

I still feel nervous.

What should I do?

Dear Advisor,

I am really good at math and we have a test soon. My friend wants to cheat off me. He says that if I am his real friend I will let him.

I don't think that is right.

What should I do?

Dear Advisor,

I am in a new class this year. My new friends in my class don't like my best friend. They say I have to choose between my best friend and them.

What should I do?

Chalkboard Publishing Inc © 2007

Canadian Health Activities Grades 4-6

Just Say "NO!"

Here are some tips on how to say "NO!" if you find yourself in an uncomfortable situation with a friend or group of people.

1. **Tip 1:**

Remember to always look the person straight in the eye, and to firmly state your position:

For example:

No, I won't do that, that's illegal!

No, I won't do that, that's dangerous!

No, I won't do that, it could make me sick!

No, I don't want to.

2. **Tip 2:**

Suggest an alternative activity or place to go. This will make it easier for others to go along with you.

For example:

Let's go to my house instead.

Let's go to the park.

3. **Tip 3:**

If you can't change your friend's mind, walk away, but let your friend know it is their choice to join you.

For example:

Well, I'm leaving. If you change your mind, come join me at _____ .

Make a list of situations where you would say "NO!"

1. _____
2. _____
3. _____
4. _____

5. _____
6. _____
7. _____
8. _____

Chalkboard Publishing Inc © 2007

Canadian Health Activities Grades 4-6

Healthy Habits: Activity Ideas

Activity Idea: Living a Healthy Lifestyle

It is important to encourage students to form healthy habits from a young age. In a whole group, review the concept of a healthy lifestyle. A healthy lifestyle includes four parts: healthy eating, regular exercise, sleeping enough and taking time to relax. List the four parts on chart paper and have students brainstorm or list things they can do to support each part.

Extension Ideas:

- Invite guest speakers from various organizations to talk to students about how they can live a healthy lifestyle.

Activity Idea: Kids Health Website

The following website is an excellent way for students to learn more about healthy habits. There is an abundant amount of information available in kid friendly language. There are also many games and other interactive activities where students can find out about: Dealing with Feelings, Staying Healthy, People Places and Things That Help Me, and Growing Up.

http://kidshealth.org/kid/

Activity Idea: Dealing With Stress

Students have to deal with stress just like adults. Many children not only have the responsibility of schoolwork, but also extra curricular activities, family chores or other obligations. With so many activities on the go, children might not have time to relax and take time for themselves. As a result, students may be tired, overwhelmed and worried if they don't complete everything they need to. Use a web graphic organizer to brainstorm ideas for dealing with stress and worries. For example, listening to music, exercising, making a schedule with a list they can check off as they complete things, or getting enough sleep.

Discussion Starters:

- What does the term "stressed" mean?
- How does it feel to be stressed?
- Do you ever worry about things? If so what are some examples?
- Who can you go to if you are worried about something?

Activity Idea: The Four Food Groups

Introduce to students that food can be classified into four food groups. Tell them about Canada's Food Guide and how there are recommended amounts of each food group that kids should eat each day. Different foods give our bodies important nutrients. Carbohydrates like potatoes, bread and cereal give energy. Proteins in meats and vegetables help make our bodies grow strong. Vitamins and minerals in fruit, milk products, and vegetables help our bones, teeth and skin stay healthy. Water helps carry all other nutrients to different areas in the body.

On chart paper post the headings of the four food groups. Have the students brainstorm food items and record them under the appropriate food group heading.

Encourage students to visit the following website and play Nutrition Café. These games offer students the opportunity to test their food knowledge.

http://exhibits.pacsci.org/nutrition/

Activity Idea: All About Calories

Introduce to students the idea that a calorie is a unit of energy that comes from the food we eat. Some foods like sugary treats have lots of calories. Other foods like celery have very few calories. Reinforce with students that calories aren't bad for you and that your body needs calories for energy. It is only when you eat too many calories and do not burn enough energy through activity that calories can lead to weight gain.

The recommended range of calories for most school-age children is 1,600 to 2,500 per day. Keep in mind that each person's body burns energy or calories at different rates depending on their size and level of physical activity. Consequently, there is not an absolute number of calories that a child should eat.

Healthy Habits: Activity Ideas

Activity Idea: Examining Nutritional Values on Packaging

Have students collect and bring in empty cereal boxes, juice boxes or other food packages. After giving some background information on nutrients, in small groups ask students to examine the nutritional level of various brands. The teacher may wish to have different groups responsible for different types of food items, including: cereal, juice boxes, snacks, etc. Next, have groups report on which items had the best nutritional value compared to similar products.

Discussion Starters:
- After learning about the importance of nutritional information, would you change your buying habits?
- What surprised you?
- How did the packaging entice consumers?
- What are the characteristics of smart consumer?

Activity Idea: Compare Nutritional Values

Ask students to bring a juice box or label from a juice container to class.

1. Ask students how pure they think their juice is by just looking at the package.
   For example, the packaging may feature pictures of fruit, or phrases like 'made with pure juice'.
2. Next, ask the students to look at the ingredients.
3. Ask students for the first two main ingredients. What are they?
4. Does their juice have pure juice as one of the main ingredients?
5. Does their juice have water and sugar and/or glucose-fructose as the two main ingredients?
6. What other ingredients are in their juices?
7. Would they recommend their juice as a healthy drink choice? Why or why not?
8. Rate the brands of fruit juices from the most healthy to the least healthy.

Repeat the above activity using snack food packaging.

Activity Idea: Be Consumer Savvy

Introduce students to the ways of being consumer savvy and particularly the ways in which packaging is designed to attract kids. Brainstorm with the class how advertisers use the design, promotion and marketing of products to sell to consumers. Have students compare similar food products using a T- chart and assess the nutritional value of the foods and beverages they enjoy.

Discussion Starters:
- Why do you think manufacturers feature famous people or cartoon characters on the front of a package? Explain your thinking.
- Do you think gimmicks such as contests, recipes or free gifts help entice consumers to buy the product?
- Have you ever noticed how sometimes the amount of a product in relation to the size of the package is off? For instance a small amount of candies are put in a big bag. Why would manufacturers do that?

Activity Idea: Create a Class Cookbook

Ask students to bring in their favourite healthy recipes and combine them to make a class cookbook.

Activity Idea: Create a Commercial

Using the commercial black line master as a guide, have students create and perform a commercial for a healthy food item.

Healthy Habits: Journal Topics

1. Why do you think it is important to eat a balanced diet?

2. How do you think what you eat affects your body and the way you feel?

3. Do you think the media influences your eating habits? Explain your thinking.

4. What do you think the differences is between a snack and a treat?

5. Do your eating habits change from when you are at home to when you are with your friends or out at a restaurant? Explain.

6. What can you do to maintain a healthy body weight?

7. Do you like to eat breakfast? Why or why not?

8. Name some of your favourite foods. Why are they your favourite?

9. Are there any foods you refuse to eat? Explain.

10. Do you check the nutritional information on the food items you eat? Why or why not?

11. Do you think convenience foods (frozen foods, canned foods, fast food) make it easier or harder to keep a healthy diet? Explain your thinking.

The Canadian Food Guide

Grain Products
5 to 12 servings

rice

cereal

bagel

bread

pasta

Vegetables and Fruit   5 to 10 servings

salad

juice

fruits and vegetables

Milk Products   2 to 4 servings

cheese

yogurt

milk

Meat and Alternatives
2 to 3 servings

egg

beans

poultry

meat

fish

peanut butter

Chalkboard Publishing Inc © 2007

Canadian Health Activities Grades 4-6

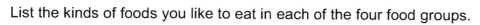

The Four Food Groups and You

List the kinds of foods you like to eat in each of the four food groups.

1. **Grain Products**

For example, 1 serving = 1 slice of bread or 1/2 cup of pasta, or 1/2 cup of rice

2. **Vegetables and Fruit**

For example, 1 serving = 1 cup of salad, 1 medium sized fruit, or 1/2 cup of juice.

3. **Milk Products**

For example, 1 serving = 1 cup of milk, 3/4 cup of yogurt, 50g of cheese.

4. **Meat and Alternatives**

For example, 1 serving = 1-2 eggs, 2 tbsp of peanut butter, 50-100g of fish, poultry or meat.

What is your favourite food group? _____

Canadian Health Activities Grades 4-6

A Healthy Eating Survey

Complete the survey to learn more about your eating habits.

	Questions	Rarely	Sometimes	Often
1.	Do you eat three balanced meals a day?			
2.	Do you eat healthy snacks?			
3.	Do you eat breakfast?			
4.	Do you eat lots of high calorie treats?			
5.	Do you eat late at night?			
6.	Do you drink at least a few glasses of water every day?			
7.	Do you eat regularly at a restaurant?			
8.	Do you eat a lot of junk food or fast food?			
9.	Do you eat when you are stressed, or upset?			
10.	Do you eat from each food group everyday?			

**Using this survey as a guide, comment on your eating habits.
How could your eating habits improve?**

_____

_____

_____

_____

Chalkboard Publishing Inc © 2007

Create Packaging For a New Cereal

Take an empty cereal box and create new packaging for an imaginary cereal. Make sure to include:

- nutritional guide
- price
- picture
- enticing slogan

Use the space below to help plan your cereal box.

Canadian Health Activities Grades 4-6

Fast Food Know How

Pretend you are going to a fast food restaurant.

1. Fill out the menu order form according to what you would want to eat. Try to be realistic.
2. Next, look up on the restaurant's nutritional guide the calories, fat grams for each item you ordered and record.
3. Add up the numbers to find out the total calories, fat grams you would eat by ordering your meal.
4. Try to plan a more nutritious meal at this fast food restaurant.

1. **Name of the restaurant:**

Menu Item	Calories	Fat Grams
Total:		

2. **Name of the restaurant:**

Menu Item	Calories	Fat Grams
Total:		

Chalkboard Publishing Inc © 2007

Brain Stretch: Fast Food Know How

1. **What surprised you?**

_____

_____

_____

2. **How do you think your ordering habits might change?**

_____

_____

_____

3. **Do you think most people realize how many calories and fat grams they are really eating? Explain your thinking.**

_____

_____

_____

4. **List some suggestions you would give to your favourite fast food restaurant to make their menu more healthy.**

_____

_____

_____

_____

_____

Chalkboard Publishing Inc © 2007

Canadian Health Activities Grades 4-6

Healthy Food Collage

Cut and paste pictures from flyers, or magazines of healthy food to create a collage. Try to include pictures from all the food groups.

1. **Write about your healthy food collage:**

_____

_____

Chalkboard Publishing Inc © 2007

Canadian Health Activities Grades 4-6

Create a poster with a message to encourage people to eat healthy!
Make sure your poster includes a message and a picture.

Plan a Healthy Eating Day!

List the different kinds of foods and portions you would eat in a day.

1.	**Breakfast**	
2.	**Healthy Snack**	
3.	**Lunch**	
4.	**Healthy Snack**	
5.	**Dinner**	
6.	**What are some healthy drink choices?**	

How many portions of each food group did you include on your plan?

Grain Products: ☐☐☐☐☐☐☐   Fruit and Vegetables: ☐☐☐☐☐ ☐☐

Milk Products: ☐☐☐☐   Meat and Alternatives: ☐☐☐☐☐☐

Explain why you think your eating plan is healthy.

_____

_____

Chalkboard Publishing Inc © 2007

Canadian Health Activities Grades 4-6

Dear Parents and Guardians,

As part of our class focus on Healthy Habits, we would like families to take part in our Eat Healthy Challenge.

The purpose of the Eat Healthy Challenge is to encourage kids to keep a healthy diet.

Challenge your child to have at least five portions of fruits and vegetables a day. Over the next five days, keep track of the number of fruits and vegetables your child eats.

Every time your child eats a fruit or vegetable colour in a box on the chart. At the end of five days complete the reflection sheet about how your child did.

In addition, whole families are welcome to take the challenge!

Your family's participation and support is greatly appreciated!

Kind Regards,

_____

Canadian Health Activities Grades 4-6

Recording Chart: Eat Healthy Challenge!

Can you eat at least 5 servings of fruit and vegetables a day for 5 days in a row?
Good luck on the Eat Healthy Challenge!

Day 1	Day 2	Day 3	Day 4	Day 5

1. **How do you think you did? Explain.**

_____

_____

Chalkboard Publishing Inc © 2007

Canadian Health Activities Grades 4-6

Recording Chart: Eat Healthy Challenge!

1. Do you think you made healthy food choices? Explain your thinking.

   _____

   _____

2. Who helped to make your food choices?

   _____

   _____

3. What was the best part about the challenge?

   _____

   _____

4. What was the hardest part about the challenge?

   _____

   _____

5. What are your favourite fruits and vegetables?

   _____

   _____

Chalkboard Publishing Inc © 2007

Canadian Health Activities Grades 4-6

CONGRATULATIONS!

Name: _____

YOU COMPLETED THE EAT HEALTHY CHALLENGE!

Chalkboard Publishing Inc © 2007

Get Enough Sleep!

People need sleep to keep healthy, happy, and able to do their best. Sometimes when people don't get enough sleep they often feel grumpy and tired. Children ages 5 to 12 need 10 to 11 hours of sleep each night!

Sleep helps your brain, so you can:

- Remember what you learn
- Concentrate and be alert
- Think of new ideas
- Solve problems better

Sleep helps your body, so you can:

- Stay healthy and be able to fight sickness
- Grow strong

Here are some sleep tips for a good night's sleep:

- Make sure you bedroom is cool, dark and quiet
- Exercise during the day
- Keep a regular bedtime
- Don't drink sodas with caffeine

Brain Stretch: Get Enough Sleep!

1. Why is sleep important?

_____

_____

_____

_____

2. How do you feel if you don't get enough sleep? Explain.

_____

_____

_____

_____

Chalkboard Publishing Inc © 2007   Canadian Health Activities Grades 4-6

Stress Busters

Stress describes a feeling you have when you are worried or uncomfortable about something. Sometimes stress may cause you to have feelings like anger, frustration or fear. Sometimes stress might be the reason you have a headache or stomachache. Some people who are stressed often don't feel like eating or can't sleep. Other people may have trouble concentrating at school, or become forgetful.

Here are a few stress buster tips:

- Talk to someone you about how you are feeling
- Take deep breaths and breathe out slowly
- Do some exercise
- Write a journal about how you are feeling and why
- Do a fun activity you enjoy

Brain Stretch: Work with a partner to complete the chart below.

Reasons Kids May Become Stressed	Things They Can Do When That Happens

Chalkboard Publishing Inc © 2007

May I Recommend...

Recommend two things people can do to have a healthy lifestyle. Make sure to explain your thinking!

I recommend...	Draw a picture.

Chalkboard Publishing Inc © 2007

Canadian Health Activities Grades 4-6

Physical Fitness: Activity Ideas

Activity Idea: Physical Fitness Survey

As a class make a list of all of the activities that students might do to be physically active. Answers will vary and might include: skipping rope, bike riding, dance lessons, walks, etc. Once the list is complete, survey students to see what activities they have tried and put tally marks beside the activities.

Discussion Starters:

- What activity is on the list that you would like to try if you haven't?
- How often do you do the activity?
- What do you like about it? How does it make you feel?
- Where do you go to these activities?

Activity Idea: Let's Get Physical!

In a whole group, show students how to feel their pulse. Next, have students do a vigorous physical activity such as jumping jacks, running on the spot, or dancing around the room to upbeat music. Once completing the vigorous physical activity, have students check to see if they feel their heart is beating faster, lungs are working harder and if their bodies feel warm. Explain and reinforce the concept to students that vigorous physical activity is important to keeping your body healthy and strong.

Discussion Starters:

- Ask students to reflect back to the physical activity survey and choose which activities would be labeled as a vigorous physical activity? Encourage students to explain their thinking.
- How did the vigorous activity make you feel?

Activity Idea: Physical Activity Challenge

Encourage students to keep physically active everyday. Ask students to take part in the 5 day Physical Activity Challenge. Each day students will record the physical activities they did along with the length of time. Challenge students to do at least 30 minutes of physical activity a day.

As a whole group, brainstorm a list of physical activities they could do. Some examples are:

- playing tag
- playing sports
- dancing
- skipping rope

- hopscotch
- dance lessons
- aerobics
- swimming

- hiking
- riding a bike
- weight training
- walking/jogging

Other Extension Activities:

- Have students use the word search black line master to create their own word search of physical activities.
- Have students conduct surveys about favourite physical activities.
- Have students create an aerobics routine to an upbeat song. Students can take turns leading the class in aerobics activities.
- Have students write a biography of a sports personality. Make sure students include why they chose that person and what characteristics that person has, to have done so well in their chosen sport.

Chalkboard Publishing Inc © 2007 Canadian Health Activities Grades 4-6

Physical Fitness: Journal Topics

1. How do you feel about gym class?

2. Do you think students should have 30 minutes of exercise at school a day? Explain.

3. You want to play a particular sport, but don't think you are good enough. What should you do?

4. Some members of your family are out of shape. What could you do to encourage them to get into shape?

5. How is being physically active an important part to healthy living?

6. If you get tired before the rest of the class during gym, what can you do about it?

7. What is your favourite sport? Explain your reasons.

8. If you could win an Olympic gold medal in any sport, which sport would you choose? Explain.

9. Sports are not the only way to be physically active. What are some other things you can do to be physically active?

10. Are you more physically active on the weekdays or on the weekends? Explain.

Chalkboard Publishing Inc © 2007

Canadian Health Activities Grades 4-6

Physical Fitness: Survey

Complete the survey to learn more about your fitness habits.

	Questions	Rarely	Often	Always
1.	What types of physical activities do you do outside of school?			
2.	Do you participate in an organized physical activity at least once a week?			
3.	Are you involved in at least one extra-curricular physical activity in school?			
4.	Do you participate in active activities (like basketball, skipping, tag, etc) during recess?			
5.	Do you and your family do physical activities together?			
6.	Do you walk or ride your bike to and from school?			
7.	Do you have fun when you are participating in physical activities?			
8.	Do you participate in any team sports?			
9.	Would you rather be active than play the computer or watch T.V.?			

Look over your responses, what responses do you have the most?

_____

What do you think this fitness survey reveals about your fitness level? Explain.

_____

_____

_____

_____

Chalkboard Publishing Inc © 2007   Canadian Health Activities Grades 4-6

Recording Chart: Physical Activity Challenge

Congratulations for taking part in the Physical Activity Challenge!

For the next five days, keep track of all the kinds of physical activity you do. Make sure you include things like walking to school, dancing, skipping rope, team sports, riding your bike, or playing outside with your friends. Can you do at least 30 minutes of physical activity a day?

	What kind of physical activity did you do?	How many minutes?
Day 1		
Day 2		
Day 3		
Day 4		
Day 5		

Reflection: Physical Activity Challenge

1. How do you think you did?

_____

_____

2. What do you enjoy about doing physical activities? Explain.

_____

_____

3. What do you not enjoy about physical activities? Explain.

_____

_____

4. If you could become an expert in two sports, what would you choose?

_____

_____

5. List the physical activities you would like to try.

_____

_____

_____

Chalkboard Publishing Inc © 2007

Canadian Health Activities Grades 4-6

CONGRATULATIONS!

Name: _____

YOU HAVE COMPLETED THE PHYSICAL ACTIVITY CHALLENGE

Chalkboard Publishing Inc © 2007

Conflict Resolution: Activity Ideas

Activity Idea: What Is Conflict Resolution?

Introduce the idea of conflict resolution to students. Conflict resolution is a process to help solve problems in a positive way. Each person involved is encouraged to take responsibility for their actions. Clear steps for conflict resolution might include:

- What is the problem?
- Listen without interrupting.
- Talk it out.
- Come up with different solutions.

Discuss and review the above process with students. Role-play different situations so students can practice walking through the process. Students should be encouraged to try to understand the other person's perspective of a conflict. The teacher may wish to use situations that are reflected in their class. Encourage students to come up with different solutions so they get in the habit that if a solution does not work, to try and find another one. In addition, post the steps for conflict resolution on the board for easy student reference.

Activity Idea: When People Feel Angry...

Explain to students that sometimes people can feel angry about a situation. Some reasons people may feel angry include:

- Something is unfair.
- Something has been taken away from us.
- Something was broken.
- Someone was mean or teased us.
- Someone is not sharing.
- Someone is in our space.

Ask students to remember a time when they felt angry. Have students explain what happened and how they handled the situation. Discuss what would be the best way to handle different situations.

Activity Idea: Acts of Kindness

Brainstorm with students what it means to be kind. Record their responses on chart paper. Next go through the student generated list and have students associate the kind of feelings they have around each act of kindness.

Discussion Starters:

- What are some ways you can be kind to others?
- How does it feel to be kind? How does it feel to be mean?

Next, have students create coupons to give out to people as an act of kindness. Coupons could be made for another student , a family member, neighbour, teacher etc.

Activity Idea: Bullying

Help students gain a clear understanding of bullying. Bullying can be described as the act of hurting someone physically or psychologically on purpose. Students should also be made aware that bullies come in all shapes and sizes. Usually someone is bullied repeatedly. Some forms of bullying include:

Physical: hitting, punching, tripping, shoving, stealing belongings, locking someone in or out etc.

Verbal: teasing, putdowns, taunting, making embarrassing remarks etc.

Relational: excluding someone from a group, spreading rumours, ignoring someone, ostracizing someone etc.

It is the hope that if students can understand what a person feels like when bullied, students will develop empathy and help stop bullying.

Chalkboard Publishing Inc © 2007   Canadian Health Activities Grades 4-6

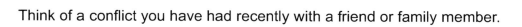

Dealing With Conflicts

Think of a conflict you have had recently with a friend or family member.

1. Describe the conflict.

_____

_____

_____

_____

2. How did you solve this conflict?

_____

_____

_____

_____

3. If you think there was a better way to solve this conflict, explain what the better way would be.

_____

_____

_____

4. If you think this was the best way to solve this conflict, explain why you feel that way.

_____

_____

_____

Canadian Health Activities Grades 4-6

Let's Solve The Problem!

Step 1

What is the problem?

Step 2

Listen without interrupting.

Step 3

Talk it out.

Step 4

Come up with a solution.

Step 5

Remember to put yourself in the other person's shoes.

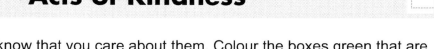

Acts of Kindness

Acts of kindness let people know that you care about them. Colour the boxes green that are examples of acts of kindness.

being bossy

sharing your snack

cooperating with others

being rude

being helpful

listening

using manners

including someone in a group

teasing someone

1. How does if feel when someone is kind to you? Explain your thinking.

_____

_____

2. How does it feel when you are kind to someone? Explain your thinking.

_____

_____

Canadian Health Activities Grades 4-6

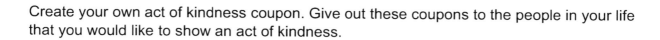

Act of Kindness Coupons

Create your own act of kindness coupon. Give out these coupons to the people in your life that you would like to show an act of kindness.

ACT OF KINDNESS COUPON

TO: _____

FROM: _____

THIS COUPON ENTITLES YOU TO:

_____

_____

ACT OF KINDNESS COUPON

TO: _____

FROM: _____

THIS COUPON ENTITLES YOU TO:

_____

_____

Canadian Health Activities Grades 4-6

Bullying: Journal Topics

What is bullying?

Do you think there are more bullies or victims in your school? Explain your thinking.

Do you think bullying is a serious problem in your school? Explain why or why not.

Do you think it helps to tell an adult about bullying? Explain why or why not.

Do you think it is possible to make a bully understand how they make their victim feel? Explain your thinking.

Have you ever witnessed someone being bullied? What happened?

Do you think that you have ever bullied someone? If so, what happened?

Why do you think someone becomes a bully?

What can each of you do to help stop bullying? Give details.

Chalkboard Publishing Inc © 2007

Canadian Health Activities Grades 4-6

Bullying: What Should You Do?

1. How do you think a person being bullied feels?

Feeling		Why?
	→	
	→	
	→	

2. Circle in **green** the things you should do when bullied.
Circle in **red** the things you should not do when bullied.

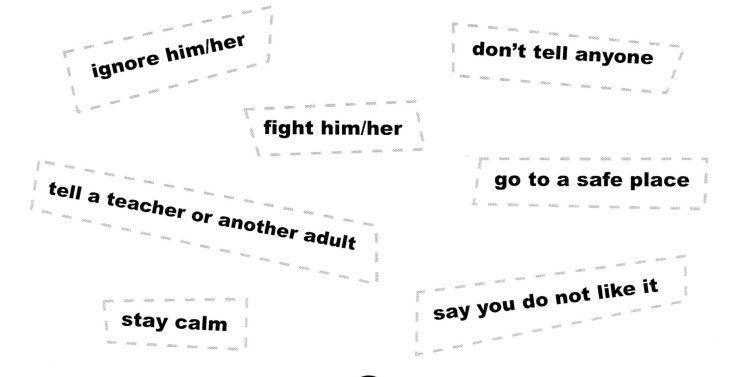

ignore him/her

don't tell anyone

fight him/her

go to a safe place

tell a teacher or another adult

say you do not like it

stay calm

Chalkboard Publishing Inc © 2007

Canadian Health Activities Grades 4-6

Stop Bullying!

What is bullying?

Bullying is when someone mistreats someone on purpose like:

- name calling or put downs.
- physical violence.
- ignoring or excluding.
- spreading rumours.

1. **What are 3 things a person who is being bullied can do?**

a. _____

b. _____

c. _____

2. **What are 3 things you can do if you see someone else being bullied?**

a. _____

b. _____

c. _____

Chalkboard Publishing Inc © 2007

Canadian Health Activities Grades 4-6

Bullying Scenarios: What Could You Do?

With a partner discuss and write a suggestion of what to do for each scenario from the perspective of: someone who is a bystander and someone who is being bullied.

Examples of bullying:	What could a bystander do?	What could the person being bullied do?
Bumping into someone in the hall on purpose.		
Calling someone names.		
Sending someone nasty emails.		
Threatening to beat up someone if they don't do what you want.		
Making someone give you money.		
Not letting someone sit next to you even though there is enough room.		
Spreading rumours about someone.		

A Letter of Advice

Choose:

- Write a letter of advice to someone who is being bullied.
- Write a letter of advice to someone who is being a bully.

Dear _____ ,

_____

_____

_____

_____

_____

_____

_____

_____

_____

_____

_____

_____

Your friend,

_____

Chalkboard Publishing Inc © 2007

Canadian Health Activities Grades 4-6

Personal Safety: Activity Ideas

Activity Idea: Role Playing

Have students work in pairs or in small groups and act out different safety scenarios to show what they would do. Scenarios might include:

- A stranger approaching you.
- A cyber pal wants to meet you in person.
- A friend dares you cross into an area that says no trespassing.

Activity Idea: Safety Tip Poster

Have students create safety posters to promote safety tips for various situations and places. Topics may include personal safety, cyber safety, safety in public places or safety tips for when doing a certain activity like swimming or riding a bicycle. Make sure to go to the website BAM! Body and Mind to find an excellent source of safety information in kid friendly language. Download safety information cards for student use.

http://www.bam.gov/

Activity Idea: Create a Safety Brochure

Have students create a safety brochure. This project could be done in small groups or individually. Headings for the brochure could include:

- What to do in an emergency.
- Home Safety.
- Public Places: Safety Tips.
- Swimming Safety Tips.
- Internet Safety Tips.

1. Demonstrate for students how to fold a large piece of paper the same way the brochure will be folded.
2. Next, show students how to plan the layout using a pencil.
   - Write the heading for each section where it should be in the brochure.
   - Leave room underneath each section to write information
   - Leave room for graphics or pictures
3. Students can then write information to fit the headings.
4. Encourage students to add eye catching pictures or graphics and slogans.

Chalkboard Publishing Inc © 2007

Canadian Health Activities Grades 4-6

Internet Safety Tips

Keep in mind the following Internet safety tips when you're using your computer at home or at school.

1. Never give out any personal Information like your name, age, address, or school.

2. Never send a cyber pal a picture of yourself without checking with your parent or guardian.

3. Never respond to messages on a bulletin board that make you feel uncomfortable.

4. Never arrange a face to face meeting with a cyber pal without checking with your parents.

5. Be aware that people on line might not be who they say they are.

6. Never set up a "user" profile to keep your personal information safe.

7. Never give out your pass word!

Brain Stretch:

1. Do you practice these internet safety tips? Why or why not?

_____

_____

2. Do you think the computer in your household should be in an area where there is no privacy? Explain your thinking.

_____

_____

3. Should your parent or guardian have access to your email account? Explain your thinking.

_____

_____

Chalkboard Publishing Inc © 2007

Canadian Health Activities Grades 4-6

Personal Safety: Journal Topics

1. Who could you turn to in an emergency?

2. Describe some situations that young people get into that are dangerous to their personal safety.

3. What would you do if there was a fire in your house?

4. What responsibilities are involved when baby-sitting or taking care of young children?

5. Why do you think it is important to practice internet safety?

6. How do you know if you can trust someone? By the way they look? The job they do?

7. What do your parents or guardians do to make sure your home is safe?

Analyzing Cigarette Advertisements

Cut out and paste in the space below a cigarette advertisement from a magazine or newspaper and answer the following questions:

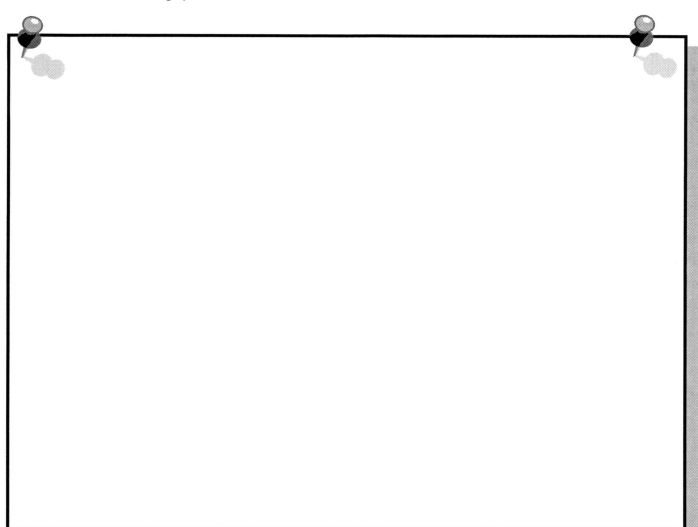

1. **What do you think the cigarette company is trying to say to you about smoking?**

_____

_____

2. **Do you agree or disagree with that message? Why, or why not?**

_____

_____

Canadian Health Activities Grades 4-6

Commercial Checklist

Write a radio or TV anti-smoking or anti-drug commercial.

My commercial is about _____

a. **My commercial tells a clear message.** ☐

_____

_____

b. **My commercial gives reasons to support my message.** ☐

_____

_____

c. **My commercial ends with a thought to remember.** ☐

_____

_____

Props:

d. **I used props to make my commercial interesting.** ☐

_____

_____

Performance Style:

e. **I practised and used good expression.** ☐

_____

_____

Chalkboard Publishing Inc © 2007

Canadian Health Activities Grades 4-6

Design a T-shirt that encourages people to stop smoking or stay away from drugs.

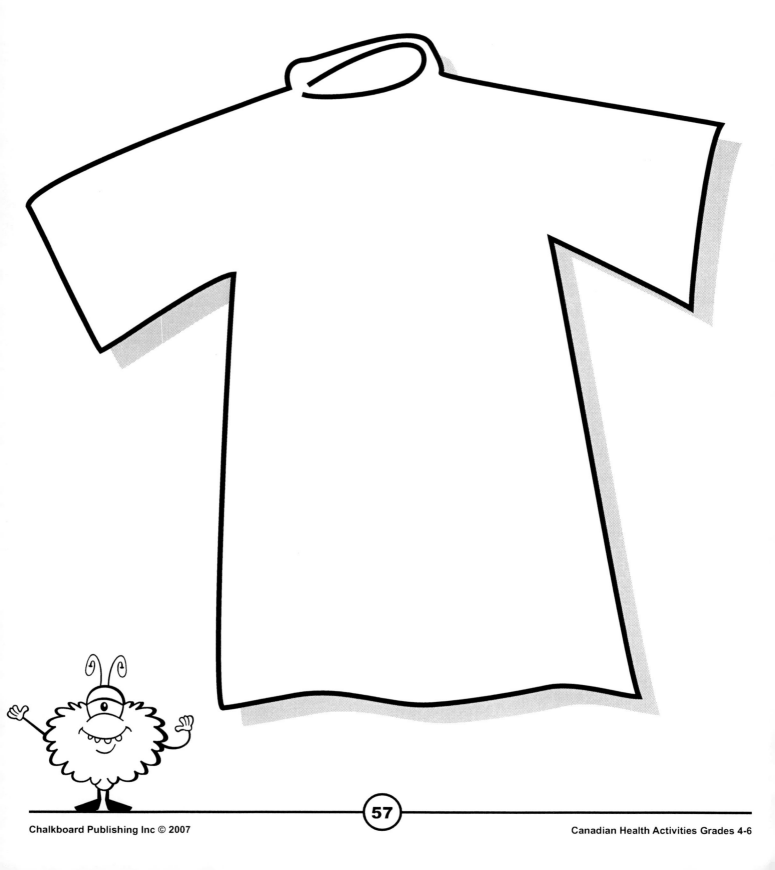

Canadian Health Activities Grades 4-6

How Do These Factors Affect You?

Think about smoking, drinking, and drugs. What influences have your friends, family, media, and teachers had on you as you develop attitudes about these things? Complete the chart by describing how you have been influenced in either a positive or negative manner.

FACTOR	ILLEGAL DRUGS	ALCOHOL	CIGARETTES
1. FAMILY			
2. FRIENDS			
3. CELEBRITIES			

Chalkboard Publishing Inc © 2007

Canadian Health Activities Grades 4-6

How Do These Factors Affect You?

Think about smoking, drinking, and drugs. What influences have your friends, family, media, and teachers had on you as you develop attitudes about these things? Complete the chart by describing how you have been influenced in either a positive or negative manner.

FACTOR	ILLEGAL DRUGS	ALCOHOL	CIGARETTES
1. MEDIA			
2. TEACHERS			

3. Who or what do you think is your strongest influence? Explain.

_____

_____

_____

_____

Chalkboard Publishing Inc © 2007

Canadian Health Activities Grades 4-6

What I Think I Know And What I Wonder About...

Write or draw in the space below.

WHAT I THINK I KNOW...

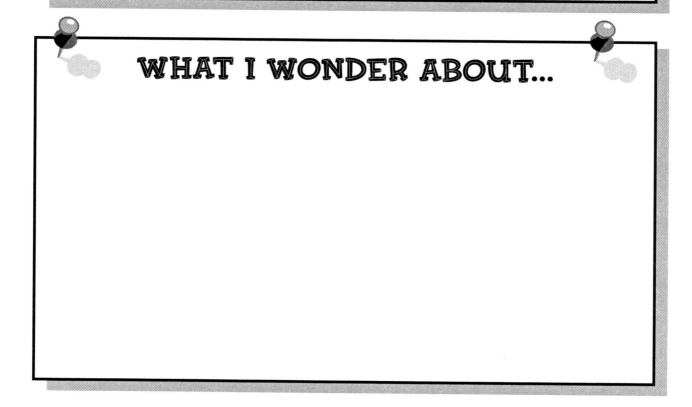

WHAT I WONDER ABOUT...

Canadian Health Activities Grades 4-6

Reporting Ideas

Non-Fiction Reports

Encourage students to read informational text and to recall what they have read in their own words. Provide a theme related space or table, and subject related materials and artifacts including, books, tapes, posters, and magazines etc.

Have students explore the different sections usually found in a non- fiction book:

1. The Title Page: The book title and the author's name.

2. The Table of Contents: The title of each chapter, what page it starts on and where you can find specific information.

3. The Glossary: The meaning of special words used in the book.

4. The Index: The ABC list of specific topics you can find in the book.

Next, discuss criteria of a good research project. It should include:

- a presentation board or other medium

- proper grammar and punctuation, for example, capitals and periods

- print size that can be read from far away

- neat colouring and detailed drawings

Oral Reports

Encourage students to talk about what they have learned and to make a presentation to the class. Here are tips to discuss with students.

- use your best voice, speak slowly, and make sure your voice is loud so everyone can hear

- look at your audience and try not to sway

- introduce your topic in an interesting way, such as: a riddle, or a question

- choose the most important information to tell

- point to pictures, a model, or diorama, as you present

Chalkboard Publishing Inc © 2007

Canadian Health Activities Grades 4-6

A Web About...

Fill in the following.

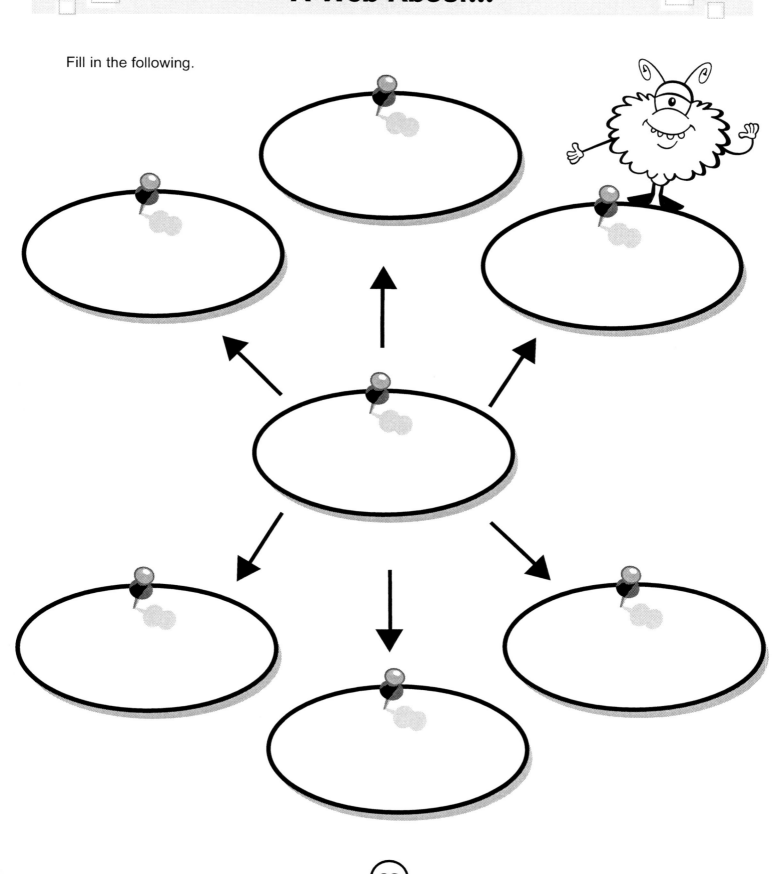

Chalkboard Publishing Inc © 2007

A T-Chart About...

Fill in the following.

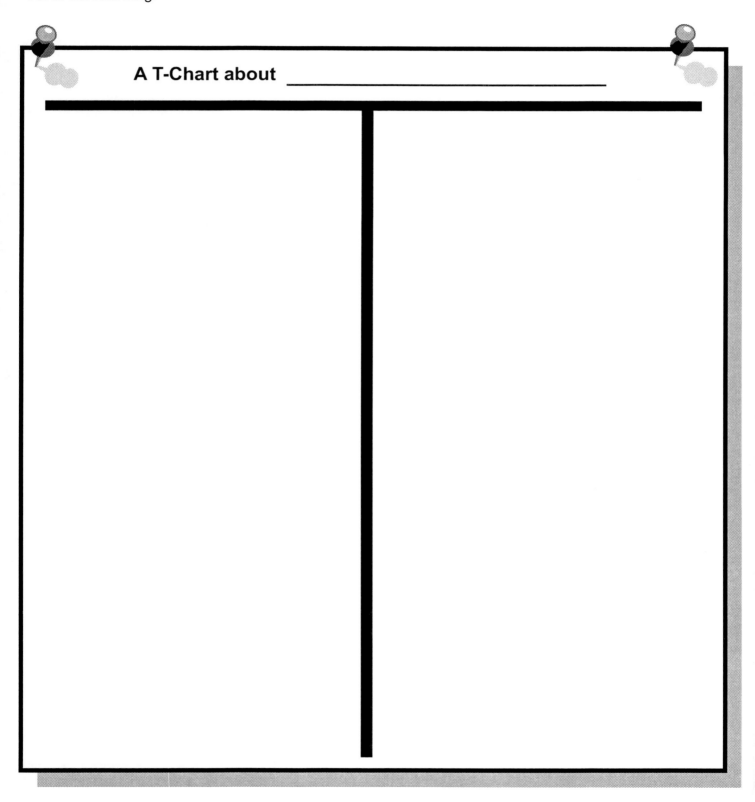

A T-Chart about _____

A Venn Diagram About...

Fill in the following.

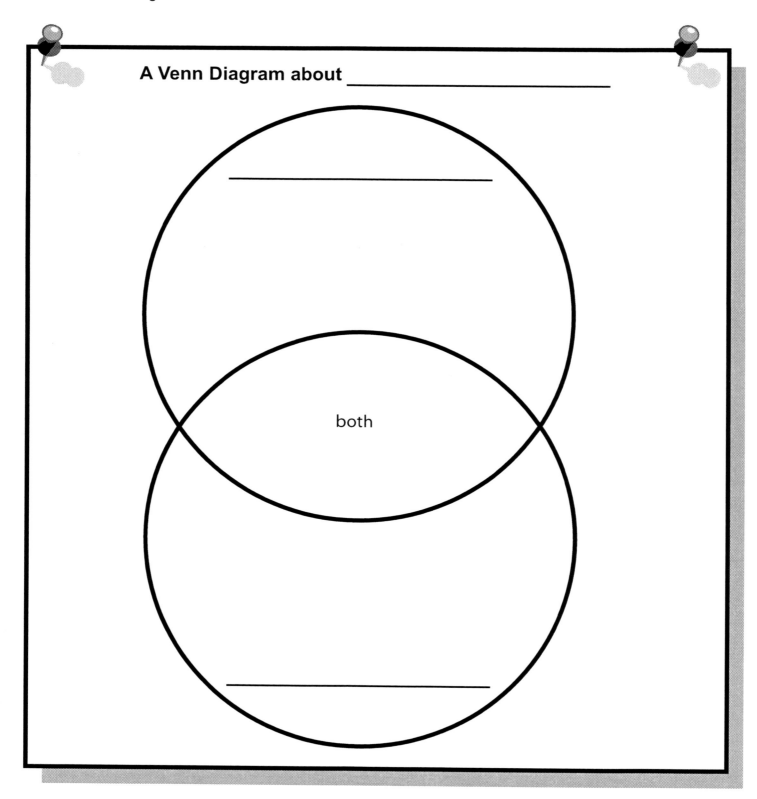

A Venn Diagram about _____

both

I am writing a letter to _____

because _____

Dear _____

_____

_____

_____

_____

_____

_____

_____

_____

Your friend,

_____

Conduct A Survey On A Health Related Issue

Survey outline

1. What is the question? _____ .

2. How many people are you going to ask? _____ .

Answer Choices	Tally Marks

3. Once you have completed your survey create a bar graph to show the information.

Canadian Health Activities Grades 4-6

Health Survey Results

Conduct a survey

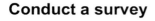 **1.** I conducted a survey about _____ .

2. I asked this question because _____ .

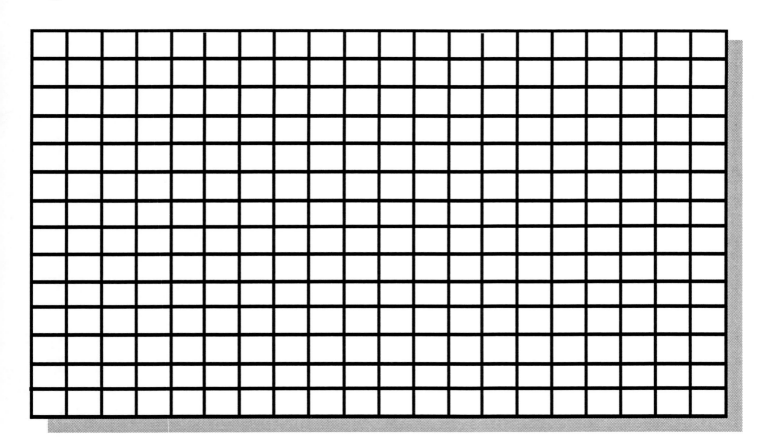

3. From the results of the survey I learned that...

_____

_____

_____

_____

Canadian Health Activities Grades 4-6

My Own Health Word Search

Create a word search and share it with your classmates.

Word Search Title: _____

Word List

-
-
-
-
-

-
-
-
-
-

-
-
-
-
-

Chalkboard Publishing Inc © 2007

Canadian Health Activities Grades 4-6

Magazine Checklist

You have been selected to create a new kids health magazine. Here is a checklist for a top quality magazine.

Magazine Title: _____

Magazine Cover:

☐ The title of the magazine is easy to read and prominent on the cover.

☐ There is an attractive illustration to let readers know the theme of the magazine.

☐ There are 1 or 2 magazine highlight statements about what is inside the magazine.

Editor's Page:

☐ The letter is addressed to the readers.

☐ The letter lets readers know why you think it is important to have a healthy lifestyle.

Table of Contents:

☐ There is a complete listing of what is in the magazine.

Advertisements:

☐ There are student created advertisements throughout the magazine for healthy products.

Magazine Plan:

☐ All the jobs on the magazine plan are complete.

Some article ideas and other columns to include in your magazine.

- Healthy Eating
- Sports Tips
- Survey Results
- Importance of Sleeping
- Anti-Bullying
- Biography of someone you admire
- Peer pressure
- Eating disorders
- Substance Abuse
- Fitness
- Internet Safety
- Recipes

Chalkboard Publishing Inc © 2007

Canadian Health Activities Grades 4-6

Magazine Plan

Group members: _____

Use the magazine plan to assign the jobs for each group member.

Job	Group Member	Complete

Chalkboard Publishing Inc © 2007

Canadian Health Activities Grades 4-6

Write A Magazine Article

Pretend you are a reporter for Kids Now! Health Magazine. Write an article to help kids understand the importance and benefits of a healthy lifestyle. Some ideas you may wish to write about include:

- Personal Safety Tips
- Importance of Eating A Balanced Diet
- Internet Safety

These are the parts of an article you need to include:

1. The **HEADLINE** names the article.

2. The **BYLINE** shows the name of the author. (You)

3. The **BEGINNING** gives the most important idea.

4. The **MIDDLE** gives supporting details about the idea.

5. The **ENDING** usually gives the reader an idea to remember.

Article Checklist:

Content:

☐ I have a **HEADLINE** that names the article.

☐ I have a **BYLINE** that shows my name as the author.

☐ I have a **BEGINNING** that gives the most important facts.

☐ I have a **MIDDLE** part that tells details about the article.

☐ I have an **ENDING** that gives the reader an idea to remember.

Grammar and Style:

☐ I used my neatest printing and included a clear title

☐ I included a colourful picture.

☐ I spelled my words correctly.

☐ I used interesting words

☐ I checked for capitals, periods, commas and question marks

Chalkboard Publishing Inc © 2007
Canadian Health Activities Grades 4-6

Health Issues: Taking One Point Of View

Write an article that gives one point of view about a health issue. Use the outline to plan your article. Some ideas you may want to write about are:

- Should students have 30 minutes mandatory exercise everyday?
- Should smoking be banned?
- Should candy and soft drinks be banned from schools?

A Statement Of Your Point Of View

Assertion	Supporting Evidence
Assertion	Supporting Evidence
Assertion	Supporting Evidence

Chalkboard Publishing Inc © 2007

Canadian Health Activities Grades 4-6

An Advertisement For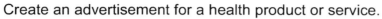

Create an advertisement for a health product or service.

Canadian Health Activities Grades 4-6

Magazine Rubric

1. Group Members: _____

_____

2. Project: _____

Criteria	Level 1	Level 2	Level 3	Level 4
Content/Information • information • accuracy • supporting details	-limited information - few supporting details	- some of the required information - some supporting details	- most of the required information - accurate and complete supporting details	- comprehensive information - very thorough supporting details
Writing Conventions • spelling • grammar • punctuation	- spelling and grammar errors in good copy - inconsistent punctuation	- some spelling, grammar, and punctuation errors in good copy	- most of the spelling, grammar and punctuation is correct in good copy	- all spelling, grammar, and punctuation are correct in good copy
Graphics / Pictures • match information • colour enhanced	- pictures rarely match information - incomplete	- pictures partially match information - some pictures are incomplete	- pictures are complete and appropriate	- pictures are outstanding and consistently match information
Overall Presentation • neat • organization	- little organization or neatness	- some organization and neatness	- general organization and neatness	- outstanding organization and neatness

3. Teacher Comments: _____

_____

_____

Chalkboard Publishing Inc © 2007

Canadian Health Activities Grades 4-6

Student Rubric

Level	Student Participation Descriptor
Level 4	Student consistently contributes to class discussions and activities by offering ideas and asking questions
Level 3	Student usually contributes to class discussions and activities by offering ideas and asking questions.
Level 2	Student sometimes contributes to class discussions and activities by offering ideas and asking questions.
Level 1	Student rarely contributes to class discussions and activities by offering ideas and asking questions.

Level	Understanding of Concepts Descriptor
Level 4	Student shows a thorough understanding of all or almost all concepts and consistently gives appropriate and complete explanations independently. No teacher support is needed.
Level 3	Student shows a good understanding of most concepts and usually gives complete or nearly complete explanations. Infrequent teacher support is needed.
Level 2	Student shows a satisfactory understanding of most concepts and sometimes gives appropriate, but incomplete explanations. Teacher support is sometimes needed
Level 1	Student shows little of understanding of concepts and rarely gives complete explanations. Intensive teacher support is needed.

Level	Communications of Concepts Descriptor
Level 4	Student consistently communicates with clarity and precision in written and oral work. Student consistently uses appropriate terminology and vocabulary.
Level 3	Student usually communicates with clarity and precision in written and oral work. Student usually uses appropriate terminology and vocabulary.
Level 2	Student sometimes communicates with clarity and precision in written and oral work. Student sometimes uses appropriate terminology and vocabulary.
Level 1	Student rarely communicates with clarity and precision in written and oral work.

Chalkboard Publishing Inc © 2007   Canadian Health Activities Grades 4-6

Class Evaluation List

Fill in the following.

Student Name	Class Participation	Understanding of Concepts	Communication of Concepts	Overall Evaluation

Canadian Health Activities Grades 4-6

Physical Activity Rubric

	Level 1	Level 2	Level 3	Level 4
Understanding of Physical Activity Concepts	Student demonstrates a limited understanding of concepts.	Student demonstrates a satisfactory understanding of concepts.	Student demonstrates a complete understanding of concepts.	Student demonstrates a thorough understanding of concepts.
Application of Skill Taught	Student applies few of the required skills.	Student applies some of the required skills.	Student applies most of the required skills.	Student applies almost all of the required skills.
Participation	Constant teacher encouragement is needed.	Some teacher encouragement is needed.	Little teacher encouragement is needed.	Student almost always participates without teacher encouragement
Sportsmanship	Student needs encouragement to be a team player.	Student will occasionally share, help and encourage others.	Student will usually share, help and encourage others.	Student acts as a team leader. Student will consistently share, help, and encourage others.
Safety	Student requires constant reminders regarding safety or the safe use of equipment and facilities.	Student requires occasional reminders regarding safety or the safe use of equipment and facilities.	Student requires few reminders regarding safety or the safe use of equipment and facilities.	Student requires almost no reminders regarding safety or the safe use of equipment and facilities.

Canadian Health Activities Grades 4-6

Thinking About My Work...

Thinking About My Work!

1. I am proud of:

_____

2. I want to learn more about:

_____

3. I need to work on:

_____

4. I will do better by:

_____

Thinking About My Work!

1. I am proud of:

_____

2. I want to learn more about:

_____

3. I need to work on:

_____

4. I will do better by:

_____

Canadian Health Activities Grades 4-6

Useful Health Websites

1. All About Kids Health
   www.kidshealth.org

2. Safe Kids Canada
   www.safekids.canada

3. An Anti-Bullying Site
   www.bullying.org

4. Stay Alert…Stay Safe
   www.sass.ca

5. The Lung Association Of Canada
   www.lung.ca/children

6. The American Dental Hygenists' Association
   www.adha.org/kidstuff

7. Health Canada: A Site For Kids
   www.hc-sc.gc.ca/english/for_you/kids.html

8. Canada's Food Guide To Healthy Eating
   www.nms.on.ca/elementary/canada.htm

9. Fire Safety Tips For Kids
   www.kfst.net/

10. Safety Tips
    www.cpsc.gov/kids/kidsafety/index.html

11. GirlSite! Network Kids
    www.girlsite.org/

CONGRATULATIONS!

Name: _____

you are a health expert!

Great work!

Canadian Health Activities Grades 4-6